The Present of the Past

Seven Stories of Faith, Devotion and

Joy in the Modern World

By Lorraine Stephens

LGS Media

❖

"The Present Of The Past"

By Lorraine Stephens

ISBN: 978-0-9745026-2-5)

Library of Congress Control Number: 2010908767

Published by LGS Media
Lorraine G. Stephens, Raleigh, NC
www.lorrainespeaks.com

Request for permission or further information should be addressed to:
LGS Media
L. Stephens & Associates, Inc.
6040-A Six Forks Road
Suite 323
Raleigh, NC 27609
Email: lorraine@lorrainestephens.com

Dedication

To Dorrian and Tiffany,
my son and my daughter,
I dedicate this book of life experiences.

You have always been there for me, without criticisms, encouraging me to continue reaching for any dreams that seemed to slip through my fingers and lifting me when I experienced any low points. You truly are a Present from my Past.

It is my hope that my life inspiring stories will one day be as meaningful to you as they have become to me.

Mom

Table of Contents

Foreword

Remember the movie "Pay it Forward"? The movie title is an expression used to describe the concept of asking that a good turn be repaid by doing a good turn for someone else.

Through <u>The Present of the Past</u>, Lorraine Stephens gently gives us several examples to reflect on how we can adjust our attitudes to evolve into our personal best.

By opening her heart and sharing both personal and touching experiences, Ms. Stephens allows us to acknowledge our insecurities and dark thoughts about our own value.

Ms. Stephens is paying it forward to us to improve our quality of life and affect all with whom we interact. Sometimes we feel we're the only ones who suffer from life's travails. Lorraine Stephens shows you that you're not alone with those 'downer' thoughts; that every negative can have a positive outcome and that you have choices on how you can view your world.

Sharon A. Hill, President
Sharon Hill International

Introduction

Even before I became a speaker I enjoyed sharing life experiences, encouraging words and motivational moments through stories. Though many of us are now on the higher end of our 'childhood years', we still enjoy stories and hold onto the messages they deliver.

This book contains seven inspirational short stories. Why seven? For years I have read that seven is the number of completion. There are seven days in a week, seven deadly sins, seven cardinal virtues, and seven years of bad luck if you break a mirror. Since this was my first book of short stories I wanted the feeling of completion. Thus seven stories.

Why inspirational? My goal, my passion, and my commitment to myself and others, is to be an inspirational woman. In my "I Wish I Had Known That Yesterday" series, I wanted to empower my readers by providing a fearless understanding of technology. I'm often thanked for doing just that. In this book I hope the stories will speak to and inspire each reader.

Each story has a message. The message that speaks to you is personally yours, reflecting your life experiences or circumstances. Why not jot the message down in the notes section at the end of the book? Your combined messages just might lead to career or personal life changes. Don't be surprised if the message is a different one when you reread the story at another time in your life. Time brings about a change. Changes bring about a different view.

Be my guest as you experience the messages delivered by Hanna of Savannah who teaches us to see things through the eyes of others; of Aunt Evelyn as you reflect on your desire to enjoy life and to develop balance; of David Neeleman when someone speaks discouraging words into your dreams and Timothy when life's desires consistently escape your grasp.

Taking a moment to read short stories, poems, or insightful thoughts is like taking a mini-vacation. I hope you will experience many mini-vacations through these stories.

Relax, read, reflect, imagine, and enjoy. That is my wish for you as you read the stories of "The Present of The Past."

Acknowledgements

My thanks seem to be endless. Bil and Cher Holton, dear friends and the editors of my very first book, once again played a key role in editing and publishing this effort. Sharon Hill, a well known speaker and author, read the stories for flow and formatting and contributed the forward. Many of my friends provided encouragement and checked with me to be sure I had not strayed from my objective, while Joan Roberts Eastman, my coach, held me to my deadlines.

Most of the art work in this book was contributed by students. Sam Stewart and Travis Marrero are both in the class of 2010 at Broughton High School, Raleigh, North Carolina and Mariah Hukins is a freshman at Duke University. My son, Dorrian Stephens, a high school teacher and football coach, even contributed his artistic gift. It was my desire to provide an opportunity for them to have their work published. Thank you so much for illustrating my stories.

My appreciation goes to Phyllis Nunn for the cover design and layout. That was not an easy task — but you did it. Let me never forget to thank, my daughter Tiffany. She has lived through the writing of every word, every brick wall that I have hit and every one that I scaled. Tiff, thanks for being my sounding board and for the weekend get away at the Blooming Garden Inn in Durham, North Carolina. That weekend truly helped me to start the finalizing process.

I could not have done this without all of you.

Featured Artist

Thank you to those that helped by contributing their artistic talents.

You Can Call Him Eddie .... Mariah Hukins

Duke University Student

Life's Like A Bubble................................. *Mariah Hukins*

Duke University Student

The View From Here .... *Sam Stewart*

Broughton High School, Raleigh NC

Ripples.. *Dorrian Stephens*

Teacher and Coach, Raleigh NC

The Present Of The Past.......................... *Mariah Hukins*

Duke University Student

You Can Do It! Let Me Help.................... *Travis Marrero*

Broughton High School, Raleigh NC

Seven Inspirational Stories

You May Call Him Eddie

It is amazing what a third grade dropout can accomplish.

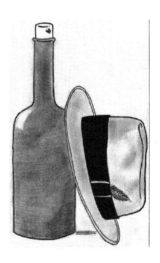

Eddie was born in a small town outside of Savannah, Georgia. He was just a little guy, a product of an economically deprived family, one of six, but full of determination. He was a product of the philosophy that was born from being told "you gotta make a hundred."

His father, a well-known entrepreneur in their small town, taught all of his children to run their own businesses. Let me hasten to add that the businesses were not necessarily 'law respected'. (That's Savannian for legal.) However, things like business practices, customer service, business procedures, business planning and more are important whether your business is legal or not. (Sounds corny, but it's true!)

You see, Eddie's family consisted of very successful multi-generational bootleggers. That is what is known in the 'crime-stopping' world as a "Crime of the Time".

Let's digress for a moment and explore bootlegging history before I share more about Eddie.... just to help you understand the context of the story. During prohibition, bootlegging was defined as the illegal distribution of liquor or other highly taxed goods. It had its place in history because it was instrumental in defeating early attempts to regulate the liquor business by taxation. Prohibition flourished during the period of 1920-1933, and by 1930 it was well organized as a large illegitimate industry.

Though his family never gained the financial status of Al Capone, a famous gangster who made a major part of his fortune through bootlegging, Eddie's family ran a business that serviced clients from Georgia through Connecticut. Of course, the Capones weren't the only ones who enjoyed the fruits of bootlegging endeavors. Other famous bootleggers were Joe Kennedy, Jay Gatsby, Tony Montana, Pablo Escobar and Bill McCoy.

Distribution was accomplished through wholesale channels by selling to owners of night clubs or through retail channels by a house-to-house delivery system to established customers. Al Capone once joked that when he sold liquor, it was called bootlegging, and when his patrons served it on Lake Shore Drive in Chicago Illinois, it was called hospitality.

Bootlegging still thrives in many areas where prohibition is still in practice. For example, a system of bootlegging untaxed cigarettes into New York City existed in the early 1970s.

> *Capone once joked that when he sold liquor, it was called bootlegging, and when his patrons served it on Lake Shore Drive in Chicago Illinois, it was called hospitality*

Okay, this brings us back to Eddie. Eddie's import vehicle was a Low Rider which is a term the highway authorities used to describe vehicles with trunks that hung low to the ground—a true sign of carrying a heavy load.

I might add that Eddie, as well as many others in his profession, had the opportunity to learn quite a bit about the legal system. Unfortunately, it was from the wrong side of the bench.

That did not stop his entrepreneurial spirit; it simply redirected his business endeavors. In the early 1940's, having relocated from Georgia to New York, he established a retail outlet for the distribution of alcohol. No, it was not a local liquor store (or ABC store for those who are familiar with this nomenclature). During that period of history, the retail outlets were called speakeasies—a fancy name for illegally operated night clubs.

Combining a flair for fashion and fine items, along with his engaging outgoing personality, Eddie's speakeasy was one of the most popular in Harlem, New York. After-hour dancing and drinking kept Eddie's Place, located in the basement of a Harlem Brownstone hopping until the break of dawn. Eddie was always dapper— sharp—and he knew how to keep a crowd entertained.

When a fire destroyed his luxurious Harlem speakeasy, Eddie shifted from the retail industry to the wholesale industry. He moved his operation to a small inconspicuous town in New Jersey. For two years he was the CEO of the largest still ever uncovered in the northeast. At least, that is what the *New York Daily News* said. In fact, that is what the judge said when he extended the invitation for Eddie to visit the state penal system for a little while.

Have you heard the saying "once an entrepreneur, always an entrepreneur"? Well, that was Eddie! After gracing the penitentiary with his presence for a while, he returned to New York and, using the business skills acquired over his lifetime, became the first African American to own and operate an express company in New York City. He was still in the distribution business, but, I might add, now it was legal.

With a fleet of seven trucks, several cars, and even bikes, Eddie provided the best in customer service with his high quality and timely deliveries. This time, driving a low rider was not a concern of the legal system. He maintained this business for over 25 years—until his death.

Though he never had formal education beyond the third grade, Eddie was definitely a natural business man. Never heard of him? He was well-known to many during his time, but you won't find him in Wikipedia.

His name? It was Fast Eddie to some. It was Dapper Dan to many. You may call him Eddie, since he was Eddie Green to his family. But to me, he will go down in history as the entrepreneur of all time. And more importantly, he will go down in history as my DAD.

You Can Do It!
Let Me Help

"You're not good enough! You can't do it!"

Encouraging words? By no means. Have you ever heard these hurtful words directed towards you? They may have come from a well-meaning friend or family member who felt they were encouraging you via the shock method. Or maybe they came from some misguided person who apparently felt he or she had been blessed with the gift of prophecy. It really doesn't matter who said it, or why they said it. What does matter is whether you allowed it to have a positive impact or a negative impact on who you are TODAY.

Recognizing and controlling the impact of negative comments is not always simple. The effects may be so deeply buried within that you don't realize they are impacting you to the degree they are. Other times you have to determine if the comment has created a LIFE NEGATIVE, and if so, how to turn it around. The most important thing is that at some point you discover the positive, and then you celebrate that positive. Today I can speak freely about how such comments adversely impacted me and about the people in my life who helped to turn it around.

Many years ago (more years than I like to admit), five weeks into my senior year in high school, I stood proudly in the office of my senior advisor—the person I looked to for guidance and assistance. It had taken over three weeks to get the appointment and I was about to explode with excitement. I wanted her to know how proud I was about finally entering my last year of high school; how much it meant to my Mom, who had raised me alone (my father left early and did not come back into my life until my late teens), and worked many long hours to get me to this point; how important it was to my family that I was preparing for college and a major in mathematics. After all, no one in my family had ever attended college. I was going to be the first. If I had worn buttons on my blouse that day, the pride swelling in my chest would have caused them to become missiles flying across the room.

In a most enthusiastic manner, I told her of the plans and dreams I had upon finishing college—plans to work with a big company as a programmer—dreams of moving my Mom out of the apartment in Harlem where we had lived all of my life into a house on a street that had grass, trees and maybe even flowers. My eyes filled with joy as I shared my plans to buy a car, knowing that Mom would no longer have to ride the subway to work, or the bus to visit my aunt in New Jersey. You see, my future, my dreams and plans, were all based on my going to college, and I was only eleven months away from that goal.

To pursue my dream I felt I needed help. Choosing a college with a good math program was key. Obtaining scholarships, grants, loans—money by any name—was mandatory. We didn't have any. So I asked my advisor for her help in researching these two areas.

For some reason I had not noticed the blank look on the face that stared back at me as I rattled off a non-stop stream of my exciting ideas and future plans. It never even dawned on me that I might be the only person in the room excited about my plans. As my advisor began to speak, her words shattered my moment and immediately impacted my life.

"Lorraine," she said, "I am not allowed to recommend colleges. That would indicate that the school system rated one college higher than another."

I felt a little of the wind leave my sails. My classmates had shared the good news of the help she had given them. I froze and remained speechless and confused as her lips began to move again. Words that would shape my life's mission passed through her lips: "…you are not college material. You won't make it. You can't do it. Why don't you try a business school? I'm sure you'll make a good secretary."

I have only a vague memory of leaving her office and passing my classmates sitting in the waiting room. I do recall that I could not look in their eyes. My head and shoulders were lowered, but not nearly as much as my spirits. That evening, as I lay in bed, the questions seemed to move through my mind like marquis lettering in slow motion. How could I have done so well in elementary, middle and high school, and not be 'college material'? How would I tell my mom that the dreams and plans were gone and that all of those hours she spent working in the factory were for nothing? And how would I ever be able to move out of our Harlem apartment? My advisor had defined who I was, what I was capable of and how my life would be—all within the span of a minute.

In spite of her comments, I applied for college and enrolled in the fall. No one knew, especially not my mom, about the secret that I carried in my heart. No one knew that I had been branded as someone who was not college material. Nor did anyone know that I felt I was cheating just by being in college. I feared the day that my secret would be uncovered.

In order to keep my secret, I silenced any questions I had. As the subject matter became more complex, the questions mounted. However, I could never let anyone know that I did not belong, that I was not college material, that I "could not do it." As I allowed the questions to mount, my ignorance grew. As my ignorance grew, my fears increased. It was really no big surprise to me when the dean called me in his office and invited me not to return in the fall.

But it did come as a surprise and a shock to a friend of the family who immediately realized that something was terribly wrong. He told me about a small college in North Carolina, sharing how he admired the way they nurtured their students, helped them find financial assistance, encouraged them to ask questions and participate in class discussions. With his assistance I completed the papers for student loans and grants, submitted my application, and that fall, found myself sitting in a classroom at St. Augustine's College.

To my regret, the 'not college material' curse had followed me across the miles. I was still sitting in class, afraid to ask questions. After all, nothing substantive had changed to give me the confidence needed. Then one day as I sat in class, bewildered over a math problem, I felt a hand on my shoulder and heard a reassuring voice say, "You can do it. Let me help". She almost sounded angelic.

She went on to explain the process of solving the problem. "First you need to see what the problem is asking. Then look at what it is going to take to solve it. Put your strategy in place. Then approach and solve the problem—piece by piece." I could not believe that someone was actually offering to help. More significantly, I was being told I could do it. This marked the beginning of a change. It signaled a new me.

The same thing happened a few days later. Again I must have had a puzzled look on my face. Again I felt a hand on my shoulder and heard a comforting voice saying, "You can do it. Let me help." These offers gradually

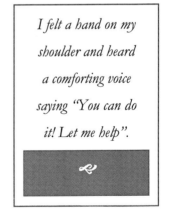

I felt a hand on my shoulder and heard a comforting voice saying "You can do it! Let me help".

changed my life. No longer was I afraid to ask questions or admit that I did not know. The 'not college material' curse was being washed away by her motivation and encouragement.

This renewed confidence was like a re-birth. It is with great appreciation that I recognize and thank **Dr. Rebecca Weatherford**, my math professor, for the role she played in this rebirth. Eventually, I began to tutor students who were having trouble and enjoyed seeing the light of confidence and understanding dawn in their eyes.

Three years after entering St. Augustine's College I graduated with honors. *I could do it! I was college material!* Now, this could be a perfect ending to this story—but it's really only the beginning. The significant part was yet to come. In spite of my success at St. Augustine, I will always remember those devastating words uttered by my high school advisor and the impact they had on me. The negative effect is obvious; however, what is not readily obvious is the positive contribution those devastating words had on my life. As a result of that experience, I am committed to eliminating fear, building confidence, and motivating those who have been made to feel that they 'can't do it', realize that they 'can do it'.

In my work as a technology consultant, I develop within each person the **MOTIVATION** to understand technology and the **CONFIDENCE** to use it as a tool **WITHOUT FEAR.**

That is the motto you will see for L. Stephens & Associates, Inc. As you read those words, can you begin to see the positive impact of that demoralizing high school experience? Without that experience, I might not have the sensitivity for people who live in fear of what they are trying to learn. So, for the thousands who have attended my seminars and workshops, we all may owe a warm "Thank You" to that misguided high school advisor—but more importantly to Dr. Rebecca Weatherford and many of the other teachers at St. Augustine's College, who took the initiative to offer help and guidance.

Many of my clients have reaped the benefits of learning how to use technology as a productivity tool. Even more importantly, they have enjoyed the journey—without fear. One of my favorite memories is of a young teacher who attended one of my classes on creating effective presentations using Microsoft PowerPoint®. As we began the class, I noticed her reluctance to ask questions or even answer one when I addressed her. This was my first clue that the Dr. Weatherford touch was needed. The experience level of those in the class ranged from intermediate to advance. Being a true beginner was very intimidating to her.

As we approached the end of the first day's class and she began to leave, I realized the need to speak to her. Touching her arm to address her face-to-face, I noticed the mist of tears in her eyes. Did I understand her feelings? Yes! Was it necessary to ask any questions? Not at all. I had already lived the moment that she was experiencing. I squeezed her arm and asked if she could give me 45 minutes of her time. She honored that request.

After we each got a cold beverage, I asked her to take a few deep breaths and relax. It soon became evident that it was not the computer's application that troubled her—it was THE COMPUTER itself. Somehow she had been led to feel she could not master the silicon thingamajig (that's computerese for Computer). I did not ask her to search her soul for the source of that feeling, I knew it would reveal itself as we progressed.

About 40 minutes into our private training time, I saw brightness in her eyes. Soon she began to get ahead of me and I lost control of her lesson—she took over! The time spent with this woman was the best 40 minutes of my day. When she asked if I would mind staying a bit longer, I jokingly said that I could spend the night if she wanted me to. We laughed and kept working.

We wrapped up our session about 90 minutes later. As she thanked me for the time we spent together, she expressed her gratitude for my patience and mentioned how she was the least computer-literate one in her family. There was pride in her eyes as she spoke of her husband, a corporate professional who spends a great deal of time on computer systems. Both he and her children "know the computer inside out", she said. The gleam in her eyes faded as she mentioned their frustration whenever they tried to teach her how to accomplish her tasks on the computer. As she continued to chat, she gave a faint smile and said, "Normally they will just ask me to move aside and they will do it for me."

Without knowing it, her family had told her "You can't do it." I'm sure it was never their intention, but their actions had stifled her and she was not able to move forward until she received a helping hand from a 'confidence restorer'. A few months after our confidence-building session, I had the pleasure of meeting her wonderful family! Isn't it interesting how such destructive emotions can unknowingly come from those who love us and feel as though they are helping us, protecting us?

Because we travel in similar circles, I often run into her. Now she glows when she talks about all of the presentations she has her students creating and how much they enjoy her class. We both chuckle when we reflect on her first day in my class. She's fine now. Mission accomplished!

Once you learn to overcome your doubts and fears, you'll consistently go into what I call your 'overcome mode' when you are faced with a challenge. The tough obstacles presented by the discouraging comments of my high school advisor, though devastating at the time, paled in comparison to challenges that I would experience later on in life. But the lessons I learned while overcoming that situation have stayed with me.

They were with me that January morning five days after my 35th birthday, and two days after accepting my first job in management, when my husband and I realized that ending our marriage was inevitable. As he packed his belongings, I wondered what on earth the life of a single parent would be like. With two children, ages three and five, I knew I had some major responsibilities ahead of me. I also knew that the new position in management was not going to be easy in the best of circumstances. I was the only woman in the management ranks in that arena. Many of my peers resented my presence and attributed my success to affirmative action. In addition, I managed 14 men who were unwilling to be managed by a woman and secretly took bets on how long I would last.

June of the same year my mom, who lived with me, was diagnosed with terminal cancer. To make matters worse, the thing I feared most occurred—my husband was not going to be an involved or supportive father. Fear, anger, depression and concerns of competence were all outposts in my mind. But these emotions were depleting the energy that I needed to use elsewhere. I had two children who were depending on me; a job in which I needed to excel in order to feed my family; and a mom who needed all of the care, support and encouragement I could give. I wasn't even sure that a 'Dr. Weatherford moment' and all of the prayers that I could muster would get me through this. "Houston, we have a problem" circled in my mind like the horses on a carousel.

But, as I said before, learning to overcome is learning to consistently overcome. Once again, as clear and as brilliant as a diamond, I heard the words: "You can do it. Let me help. First you need to see what the problem is asking. Then look at what it is going to take to solve it. Put your strategy in place. Then approach and solve the problem— piece by piece." This advice, given over 12 years ago, was still

> *"First you need to see what the problem is asking. Then look at what it is going to take to solve it. Put your strategy in place. Then approach and solve the problem—piece by piece."*
>
> **Dr. R. Weatherford**

applicable. In fact, it repositioned me to 'overcome'. Once I broke that bigger than life problem up into smaller pieces, it became manageable. Not easy—but manageable. I think of it as my 4-R period:

Relocate: I sold my home and moved my family to a less expensive part of the country. It was a sheer blessing to find that the less expensive location was far better for raising my children. It provided a built-in community of children and stay-at-home moms who loved my children. This gave me the time needed to care for my mom. The children loved the new environment and appreciated all of their new friends. The time that my children and I spent together became quality time.

Retool: The job—you know the one with the unsupportive peers—I gave it up! Another wonderful organization offered me a position that was very well suited for my technical and management experience. My gender did not play a role in their selection and my peers admired and respected my contribution. It was a wonderful switch from a negative environment to a positive one.

Relocate
Retool
Reevaluate
Remove

<u>Reevaluate</u>: My priorities had become jumbled because of my needs. Mom was not going to spend many more years with me so I needed to jump off of the money boat and get back in the family boat. I did just that. It would take time to seek out the proper medial care, to provide the attention that she needed and enjoy our closing moments together. Thank goodness for this reevaluation.

<u>Remove</u>: The anger that had built up in my life had to go. It caused me to constantly think of all of the 'should haves' and 'could haves' from the past. Folks, that kind of second guessing and

self-criticism will kill you! By purging myself of the anger I had toward my ex-husband, my previous job situations, and the doctors (yes, I was even angry at them for not healing my mom), my positive mental health soared. I was able to accept and enjoy life again.

Let me not understate the help I received while going through this difficult period. It came from many friends and family members to whom I will forever be indebted. In their very own way, they kept their comforting hands on my shoulder while telling me "You can do it. Let me help."

Fortunately, my son and daughter, Dorrian and Tiffany, are encouragers. Without knowing the details of the awful high school experience that sensitized me toward criticism, they understood my sensitivity to negative comments. They have learned how to recognize when negative or degrading comments are directed at them—regardless of how cleverly they are disguised. In addition, they know the positive power of the tongue and they strive to exercise that power in a constructive manner. I proudly observe their response and reaction to problems. They don't fear tackling them because they have been instilled with self-confidence.

Thank you, Ms. High School Advisor for giving me one of the first big lemons of my life. (Yes, I have forgotten her name. After all, there is a limit to just how nice I want to be). But above all, thank you Dr. Weatherford, for revitalizing my life and showing me how to enrich the lives of others. I carry your words "You can do it. Let me help." with me every day. I repeat those seven golden words to those I strive to make more comfortable as they embrace the use of technology. You have definitely helped me make lemonade out of many of life's lemons.

From *this* woman's perspective, whatever challenges you may find yourself facing, know that "you can do it!" When an unpleasant experience generates a negative-turned-positive result, learn from it, express your appreciation and move on. It is for this reason I have shared my life-changing experience and its positive results

Motivation and confidence, without fear

with you. Hopefully it will encourage you to do the same. I feel very fortunate in my work to have the opportunity to help develop within each person the MOTIVATION to understand technology and the CONFIDENCE to use it as a tool WITHOUT FEAR.

It is a pleasure to pass on to you the torch of

helping another who may be a bit reluctant (or just plain scared) to ask for assistance. Simply rest your hands on their shoulder and tell them, "You can do it! Let me help."

Ripples

In 1906 the Boys Clubs of America was founded to help children from all backgrounds become quality citizens and leaders. Do you think they knew they would create such an outstanding list of alumni?

- Bill Cosby
- Jackie Joyner-Kersee (yes even a girl!)
- Denzel Washington
- Brad Pitt
- Michael Jordan
- Neil Diamond

Maybe the Boy's Clubs' executives didn't know the extent of their influence, but surely they hoped for it.

Do you think that Anne Sullivan had any idea of the impact she would have on the world when she worked with a little girl named Helen Keller who was blind and deaf? Did you know that Helen Keller was the first deaf-blind person to earn a Bachelor of Arts degree? Think of the ripples she caused in people's false expectations of the role the sight-challenged and hearing impaired can play in our society.

You've no doubt heard of Jackie Robinson, baseball Hall of Famer and the first "colored" player to earn the National League's MVP Award. When Branch Rickey, the owner of the Dodgers, invited Jackie Robinson to be on the team, he told him that for three years he would have to turn the other cheek and silently suffer all the vile things that would come his way. It wasn't Jackie's nature to do that. He was a fighter, a proud and competitive person. This was a man who, as a lieutenant in the Army, risked a court-martial by refusing to sit in the back of a military bus. That took courage, don't you think? And courage seemed to define Jackie Robinson's life.

But when Rickey read to him from *The Life of Christ,* by Bishop Fulton Sheen, Jackie understood the wisdom and the necessity of forbearance. Because of his success as a "colored" player, the path for many was paved. The ripples that a boy from Cairo, Georgia created in both the military service and the world of baseball reached all over the world.

All of these incidents were single actions by ordinary people—intended for those they were addressing—but they impacted thousands.

As a little girl I enjoyed going to the lake with my cousins and friends to skip rocks across the water. I thrilled in knowing that the calm glass-like surface would be forever altered when just a little stone pierced its top. A little circle would form—then a bigger circle would form—and a bigger one. I knew that the circles continued to form even beyond my being able to see them.

As my cousins and friends released the smooth stones from their hands, they were sure to hold them just right so that they could get the maximum number of skips from the stones. (If you've never skipped stones across a lake or pond, you've got to find a body of water after you read this segment and skip a few flat stones. Otherwise, your childhood won't be complete!)

It was a competitive game for them. I, on the other hand, was counting the number of

ripples with a fascination for the fact that they kept growing and expanding. It seems like they never stopped having an impact on the water. As they grew I watched, imagining the ripples getting bigger and bigger, picking up strength and eventually spilling over into a larger body of water. In my mind's eye, I saw them eventually entering the ocean.

There was no doubt in my mind that they would someday become a mighty wave. In fact, I thought that someday, when I would go to Coney Island, a popular beach on the Atlantic Ocean in New York, I would run into the water and ride the waves, knowing for sure they were created by the stones my cousins and I had thrown in that small body of water years ago. (If you think that sounds farfetched, I've got to ask you if anyone knows where ripples stop.)

Imagine a little girl (that would be me) from the inner city (that would be New York) thinking there was even a chance she could impact the ocean. What an unreasonable dream! What a wild imagination! What a ripple effect! The possibilities seemed incredible until I found myself in the profession of delivering technology training to teachers in the North Carolina school systems. As I helped them understand how to manage information in spreadsheets, professionally format reports, develop databases and analyze data, I realized I was creating ripple effects. I was equipping them to better instruct the students in their classrooms.

I realized that every stone I threw in their instructional lake would ripple throughout their schools and school systems. But the ripple effect did not stop there; it would have an impact on not only the students, but their families as well. Suddenly I realized that my ripples were actually impacting families, neighborhoods and communities. That's an incredible thing. A greater feeling of joy overcame me as I realized I was impacting the future. My interest in the future is the same as Charles F. Kettering's, who proclaimed his interest in the future "...because I'm going to live the rest of my life there."

To me, whether the ripple effect is created by a stone tossed in a lake or a comment spoken by a teacher, a parent or a minister, the result is the same—greater communities are impacted. What a feeling of empowerment—and what a responsibility. Once a ripple starts, once an idea is set in motion, it has an ever growing impact.

Are you aware of the ripples that you're creating? Every time you do something that has an impact on a person, you potentially change society. Did you know that? A kind gesture in the grocery store to let someone get in line in front of you;

advice given to a young person trying to decide how to handle a sensitive situation; a note of congratulations sent to someone who has experienced an accomplishment—these are all examples of small acts of kindness that create ripples. It's from numberless acts of courage and integrity that human history is shaped. Take a deep breath! No matter who we are, or what we have been or where we have come from, we can send ripples of hope, joy and peace.

Small acts of kindness create ripples.

I don't know about you, but teachers and coaches who work with children and young adults never cease to amaze me. Tirelessly they work to shape the individual who sits before them. With a determination to help others improve, gain skills and wisdom and develop respect for others, they pour their hearts and souls into their jobs. When I am in their presence, I can almost hear the sound of the rushing water as their ripples form waves of hope and happiness.

But just as the person tossing a stone only sees the symmetrical ripples immediately caused by the toss, life's 'ripple makers' can often only count the immediately visible ripples they create —the changes they can see in the student's eyes and behavior:

- the student who begins to speak with pride and respect instead of profanity crammed expressions;
- the tall lanky girl who once stood with a slouch, ashamed of her physical appearance, now begins to stand tall, showing signs of self confidence;

- a failing student who develops an interest in school and makes the honor roll and stays in school.

Those are immediate and visible changes these 'ripple makers' can observe.

But one day, long after the initial ripple effect, the young man who began to speak without the use of profanity might become an attorney working for grass root causes; the young lady who grew to stand tall in confidence might become a surgeon providing services to those who are not able to afford them; and the failing student who turned his grades around just might be the next National Teacher of the Year. The ripples have become powerful waves. They have created unbelievably large and magnificent beliefs, philosophies, and world views that are beneficial to many—far beyond the awareness of the initial ripple maker.

Often I stop to reflect on my life today. Am I still tossing positive, success-oriented stones into a pond? Do I continue to create positive, life-affirming ripples? I truly hope so. Opportunities to help young adults with their leadership skills, mentoring single moms trying to hold it all together, or supporting someone just getting started in business are among the stones I toss today. Not only is it personally rewarding while I am with them, it is a moment of total happiness later when they call to share news about promotions, challenges that they stepped up to, or even to ask for further guidance and advice.

How, you ask, do you create positive life-changing effects? It's really quite simple.

- When your goal is to increase a person's comfort level with an assigned task, throw in a stone of **C**onfidence.

- If your goal is to encourage people to try something new or to show them how, toss in a stone of **M**otivation.

- When you want to help someone understand or learn something new; toss a stone of **K**nowledge.

- If your goal is to contribute to their leadership skills, toss a stone of **E**mpowerment.

Before you even think about putting this chapter aside, reflect for a moment on the number of people you have knowingly mentored, helped, listened to or taught. Then think of the young men and women who just wanted to:

+ be in your presence
+ hear your conversations
+ imitate your style of dress and your mannerisms
+ or repeat your quotes

They are becoming stronger, more knowledgeable, more determined, and more aware. This will lead to the significant contributions that they will make as they add their ripples to your ripples.

I'd like to share more about the privilege of creating ripples, if you can stand a little more excitement. Educators and those who work with our youth – men and women from all walks of life – I salute you. You prepare our youth and others for greater service to humankind. You know the value of *TOUCHING someone* — and I see you willingly doing just that. It is wonderful that you see the immediate impact of your ripples; however, you may never know how far reaching they really are. Rest assured, your influence will ripple through the centuries.

I keep smooth stones around me. You'll see them in my purse, on my desk, even in my car. They are reminders of just how powerful our influence is and how we effect change. Accept my invitation to keep a stone with you as a reminder of

* those you have touched
* those you can touch
* and those you will never know you touched.

Thank you for tossing the 'stones' that create the ripples that help transform people's lives.

Who's Defining You?

If I were a British gentleman (or a New Yorker bellman or a rodeo cowboy), I would tip my hat to each of you who have taken it upon yourself to travel an unfamiliar path—or the road less traveled, as it is known today. Many of you are making brave and important decisions to venture out into the turbulent waters of business, education, entrepreneurship and corporate landscapes. That decision alone speaks volumes about your desire to grow professionally, but even more significantly—personally.

To reach this point in your life's journey, there had to be times that you looked back and asked yourself

- Who is determining MY goals?

- Who is creating MY dreams
- Who is influencing MY decisions?
- Who is defining ME?

Those questions may seem trite or trivial until you carefully examine issues such as

- what has happened in your life;
- what is currently happening in your life;
- where you want to go from here.

Then you realize it's your roadmap you're creating and following—or not following.

As children we are defined by family, friends, teachers and so many others. It amazes me when I hear parents forecast the future of a new born baby. Their comments are humorous once you think about it. How many times have you heard comments such as: "You can tell by the length of her fingers that she is going to be a professional piano player" or "Look at the intensity of his eyes. There is no doubt that he will be a lawyer." One of my favorites is, "He has taken apart everything we have given him. He is destined to be an engineer."

Amazing, isn't it? A baby in a basinet with a career already planned. The seeds of defining who or what we will be are being planted into our minds as we grow.

By the time we become adults, the influences have come from everywhere: teachers, friends, well-wishers, and not so well-wishers. We constantly have to ask ourselves life-defining questions. Who is defining me? What impact have I allowed that to have on my life? What can I do with that experience? What lessons can I learn from this?

Let me introduce you to 13 people whose names are probably familiar. If by chance, as you scan the list that follows, you notice a name that is familiar, please put a check mark next to the name. If you see a second familiar name, check that one also. If by some miracle I mention a third and fourth and fifth who are familiar, check those also. Here goes. See how many you recognize:

☐   David Neeleman

☐   James Joyce

☐   Walt Disney

☐   Elvis Presley

☐   John Grisham

☐   Wilma Rudolph

☐   F. W. Woolworth

☐   Dr. Seuss

☐   Charles Schulz

☐   Vince Lombardi

☐   Oprah Winfrey

☐   Michael Jordan

☐   Mary Kay Ashe

Did you check any? Perhaps one, or maybe even two? Chances are you checked several of them, when actually you should never have heard of any them. However, there are defining moments in these people's lives that had the potential to 'make or break' them. These names are familiar to you because you've seen the impact of their life choices and heard their stories. They are all movers and shakers, as the saying goes. But they each began as a 'regular person' with no idea of becoming world renowned.

Even though they come from a variety of backgrounds, and their impact spans a range of fields, they all share some very powerful beliefs that we can emulate. For example,

1. They were all entrepreneurial thinkers.
2. They chose who and what would influence them—and did not allow outside negative opinions to define them.
3. They all chose to accept criticism as encouragement.

Your self-definition depends on your ability to adopt these kinds of beliefs, so why not begin immediately to incorporate them? Let's look at how you can start right now.

Become an entrepreneurial thinker

What does it mean to be an entrepreneurial thinker? Simply stated it means observe and learn what others do. Then find a different way to do it—a better way.

That is exactly what David Neeleman, CEO of Jet Blue Airlines, did when he started Jet Blue. Even though it was a time when airlines were going bankrupt, Mr. Neeleman decided to start an airline of his own. Needless to say, he was discouraged by many. "The timing is bad." "The economy will cause you to fail." Over and over, he heard these concerns from 'experts' who tried to get him to see the error of his plan.

David Neeleman, however, felt that he had found a different way and better way to run an airline. He decided he would provide the very best in customer service. After all, that was not necessarily a priority with the other airlines. When asked about starting an airline, he said, "We are not in the airline business, we are in the customer service business." In fact, he made it a commitment to fly frequently as a passenger on his own airline to assure that service excellence was being provided.

In order to provide customer service excellence, Neeleman offered economy fares, plush leather seats, 24 channel satellite TV on each flight and no Saturday night stay requirements.

Another element of his plan was to avoid the cost of building reservation centers. By hiring stay-at-home moms and placing a computer in their homes, not only did he avoid the brick and mortar costs (which would have to be passed on to the consumer), he helped families have a better life by allowing moms to stay with their children. Thanks to his entrepreneurial thinking, Jet Blue was a success.

Mary Kay Ash, a name familiar around the world, was upset with the way she had been treated in the male-dominated business world. She began to make a list of all the negative and positive things she'd seen working for her previous employer (Stanley Home Products). As she pulled all her ideas together, she discovered she had the perfect plan for a successful company. Observe and learn what others do, then find a way of doing it better. By implementing her business plan, she impacted thousands of business owners around the world with Mary Kay, Inc.

Select your influencers—Don't let them select You

During a brief period of my son's high school days, I noticed he was vulnerable to falling prey to some influences I did not feel were to his benefit. He wanted to act like *them*, talk like *them*, and be like *them*. Instantly I had to assume the role of the "persuader" and help him be more selective of his influences. (You know, help him pick his "*thems*" more wisely!)

At the time, he was not necessarily excited about my position, but he never gave me any trouble about it. Then, fast forward to his high school graduation. As we stood in the reception area together, he thanked me, commenting that none of the young men he had partnered with at that time graduated from high school. Naturally that made my eyes sweat. (That is my indirect way of describing a mother's tears ☺).

Today he is a teacher at his alma mater high school, as well as a football and softball coach. He is known for the impact he has on the students who fall within his sphere of influence.

Back when I was convincing him to choose better "*thems*," I shared stories about others who made wise choices in their influencers. I mentioned Wilma Rudolph, who won three Olympic gold medals in 1960 despite having polio as a child. During an interview she said, "The doctors told me I would never walk again, but my mother told me I would. So I believed my mother."

Wilma Rudolph is a wonderful example of the power of choosing to select your influences—and not letting them select you.

Accept criticism as encouragement

Think back on the times when a single criticism changed your entire day, or worse yet, your mindset. When you relinquish control of your mind and emotions to another person, you have just given away your power. Let me restate that. When you relinquish control of your mind and emotions to another person, you have just given away your power. You have allowed them to have an extreme influence in your life. Is that what you want to do? Is that how you want to live your life?

We can learn something about this as we explore other names on the list of familiar people whom you would never heard of had they made different life choices. Each of them turned the criticism they received around and chose to stand in the truth of who they really were.

Nearly everyone has heard of Disney World, and is familiar with Mickey Mouse and Disney founder, Walt Disney. But not everyone knows Walt Disney's story. If he had listened to those who criticized him, there

> *When you relinquish control of your mind and emotions to another person, you have just given away your power.*

would not be the much loved Disney Land and Disney Worlds. Just as an example of the many critics he dealt with, consider this story. When presenting his idea of a theme park to the city leaders in Burbank, California, he was told that it was too much of a 'carny' atmosphere for such an upscale area. Thank goodness Walt accepted criticism as encouragement.

Or how about Elvis Presley? When Elvis first appeared on the stage of The Grand Ole Opry, he was advised to go back to driving a truck. Had he followed that advice, there would be no Elvis and no Graceland legend we have today. He simply took criticism as encouragement.

Everyone who recognizes the name Vince Lombardi knows that he was considered one of the greatest, if not the greatest, football coaches of all time. When coaching the Green Bay Packers, not only was he known for his knowledge of football, but for the highly motivational speeches he delivered to his team in the locker room. As a matter of fact, he became one of the most highly sought after motivational speakers of our time. Who would have thought that early in his career he was told he had "minimal football knowledge," and he "lacked motivation?" Strong criticism! But Vince turned criticism into dynamism. One of his most famous quotes says it all: "It's not whether or not you get knocked down; it's whether or not you get back up."

Let's look at one more example. When I reflect on the entrepreneurial thinking of Frank W. Woolworth, it makes me smile. Not thought of as the sharpest crayon in the box by his boss, Frank was dubbed as one of those who "lacked sense" because of his nervousness. You see, Frank's nervousness made it virtually impossible for him to remember prices. Frank, however, refused to accept the diagnosis of "lacking sense." He took that harsh criticism as encouragement.

Believing he could excel in the dry-goods world, he started his own retail business where the prices would be easy to remember. There were only two price points in Frank's store. An item either cost a nickel or it cost a dime. Now don't get ahead of me! Yes, you guessed it. That philosophy was the beginning of Woolworth's Five and Dime Stores. Can you imagine the chagrin of his old boss when the first Woolworth store opened? The turn-around came because Frank Woolworth accepted criticism, and turned it into encouragement.

As for the others who were on the list, they all became household names because of their ability to transform criticism into encouragement. James Joyce, (author of <u>Dubliners,</u> <u>Ulysses</u> and

<u>Finnegan's Wake</u>), Dr. Seuss (author of the famous <u>Cat in the Hat</u> series and numerous other children's books), and John Grisham (author of legal thrillers such as <u>The Client</u> and <u>The Chamber</u>) experienced many rejections before their books began to get published. Charles Schulz's drawings failed to make his high school yearbook and his original comic strip "*Li'l Folks*" was rejected several times before being picked up and re-titled "*Peanuts*".

Michael Jordan was cut from his high school varsity basketball team for being too short. We all know about his basketball success! Oprah Winfrey was told she was too dark to be a TV talk show host. Today she is the most successful talk show host in American TV history—not to mention her success as a movie producer and business executive.

Successful people decide which opinions to believe and find a way to reframe criticism as encouragement. What about you? What criticism can you think of that encouraged you to excel? What criticism can you think of that you're allowing to stop you from venturing into a different territory?

So there you have it! Three powerful guides that can transform you into the winner you are: become an entrepreneurial thinker; select your influencers—don't let them select you; and accept criticism as encouragement. So you might be wondering,

> *Become an entrepreneurial thinker; select your influencers—don't let them select you; and accept criticism as encouragement.*

have any or all of these three beliefs played a key role in my own life? You betcha!

I remember my days as a technical trainer in the corporate world. Three days of training was allocated to each network package that was sold. This gave the customer just three days to learn sixteen applications and network operation. Though it made good business sense, it was not necessarily beneficial for the clients. Watching their faces as they tried to absorb so much information so fast, I felt their frustration and empathized with their expressions of defeat.

This fed my plan for providing training outside of the confines of the corporate box I was in. The difference was obvious: I did not have huge overhead as the key driver of my time and prices. I could allocate more hands-on time for going through materials. Every question was encouraged and patient responses became a trademark. As a result, I have grown the Education & Technology Group of L. Stephens & Associates, with a commitment to "Develop within each person the Motivation to understand technology, and the Confidence to use it as a tool Without Fear." I attribute my success to the three powerful beliefs I have shared as the basis of this chapter, and to Hanna's silk hankie—but that's another story (see the chapter entitled "*The View From Here*").

I always will remember the high school advisor who told me I was not college material. In spite of my honor society involvement, high grades, and extracurricular activities, she discouraged me from attending college and encouraged me to go to a trade school. Though I had nothing against trade schools, trade schools did not offer a degree in mathematics. That degree was my goal. So I traded her advice for my intuitive sense of purpose. I let *me* define *me.*

Her lack of confidence in my ability and her criticism of my goals lit my inner fire. When I graduated from college with a major in math and a minor in physics, it took every bit of restraint not to seek her out and proudly inform her how mistaken she was. However, now that I have matured, I'm actually grateful to her. Her criticism motivated me to keep running the race until I crossed the degree finish line.

Let me extend a challenge to you today. On the following page is a commitment I ask that you make to yourself. Please take some time to read it, think carefully about your responses and sign your commitment.

Name _____.

- Think of one criticism which has you sitting on the fence, avoiding a decision. Write it down.

  _____

  _____

- If you took this decision on with a vengeance, what would it encourage you to do?

  _____

  _____

- Are you willing to make the decision and take it on with a vengeance?
  Yes ☐ No ☐

  If you responded "Yes" please sign and date this page.

  Signature _____ Date _____

Now copy your signed commitment to yourself and place it in a meaningful place. (I place papers in my Bible or some other book I enjoy reading. Sometimes I even tack them on the bathroom mirror.) I would encourage you to place this written commitment in one of your favorite spots and see where you are with transforming this criticism within the next 12 months.

If you would like me to be your conscience, send me a copy of your signed page and I will gladly follow up with you.

Send it to: Lorraine@lorrainestephens.com

Subject Line: My Commitment to Self

Or mail it to:

Lorraine Stephens
6040-A Six Forks Road, # 323
Raleigh, NC 27609

As one who defined herself from the inside out,
Mary Kay Ash stated it so well when she said:

"Do you know that within your power
lies every step you ever dreamed of stepping,
and within your power
lies every joy you ever dreamed of seeing?
Within yourself
lies everything you ever dreamed of being.
Dare to grow into your dreams
and claim this as your motto:
Let it be me."

Mary K. Ash

I sincerely wish you the best in taking control of
"Who's Defining You."

The View From Here

What do you see from where you sit today? What is the view from there? Let me invite you to stand and absorb your surroundings. Don't hold out on me. Stand so you can move around a bit! Go ahead. Look around the room. Go take a look outside. Then come back in, have a seat and think for a moment as I share a story with you about the view from here. This story changed the way I see so many things. I'm hoping it will change the view for you, too.

Let me begin by describing the setting for my story.

Things could not have been more beautiful. I was visiting one of the wealthiest women in the suburbs of Savannah, Georgia. Let me take a moment and describe this place to you. In fact, I invite you to imagine yourself there with me. Plush, soft silk cushions of peach and teal adorned the white oversized rattan sofa on the patio. An ebony hand-carved table created a marked but well designed contrast to the softness of the cushions. Tall, lush airy green palms grew from fine clay pots to shade the patio and give the feeling of a tropical island. A tall waterfall trickled water at just the right pace to create a song. A framed frayed peach and teal silk hanky hung next to the waterfall.

It was breathtaking. Can you see it? Give yourself a moment now to see it with me. Capture the essence of the scene I am describing. Can you imagine the beauty of the palms? Can you picture that waterfall? It was incredible!

But all of this paled in comparison to the perfectly manicured four-acre lawn and golf course stretching beyond it. Weeping willows, magnolia trees and an apple tree added both strength and gentleness to the sprawling green lawn. Are you still with me? If so, imagine taking a deep breath and getting a whiff of roses, gardenias and peonies sending out a perfumed fragrance—as you tried to just take it all in. And listen . . . can you hear the brooks of running water and see the benches placed in strategic locations, perfect accents to an already luxurious lawn? They seem to call out with an invitation to sit down, relax and be still. Nothing was missing. Nothing!

All of this paled in comparison to the sprawling three-story brick home that it surrounded. The house was not ostentatious (hard to believe, isn't it?). In fact, it was built with extremely good taste, warm and welcoming. Looking around the beautiful patio area, I realized I was surrounded with the finest of everything you could imagine. I sat down with Hanna, the proud homeowner who was relaxing in a swaying hammock while enjoying the afternoon breeze. She seemed truly interested in sharing a bit about life with me as we began our conversation together.

"Hanna" I said, "you have the most magnificent view from here. Regardless of where I look, the view in every direction has been beyond description. I'm sure you designed it that way."

"Lorraine" she whispered in a soft but joyful voice, "You aren't seeing the real view from here. Come walk with me and let me describe what I see when I look around. It comes in scenes, each one more meaningful than the last.

As we walked together, she began to describe the first scene, overlooking a perfectly manicured golf course. "When I look over here," she exclaimed, "I don't just see the golf course, the lake, the sand traps, and the golfers. No. I also see long rows of cotton, tobacco and corn. I watch in awe as men with big strong backs drag large bags filled with what they are harvesting. Sweating, hot, thirsty—but unable to rest. I see women wearing bandannas and straw hats to keep the smoldering sun off of their heads. My ancestors worked this land during the days of slavery."

She continued as she described the second scene overlooking an orchard and garden area. "Looking a little further," she said, "I see sharecroppers picking apples, digging potatoes and farming. They are poor, but they are free and they are singing. Do you hear them, Lorraine?

We both know they will not have much left when the landowner claims his share, but they have hope, they have joy and they have dignity."

> "*They have hope.*
> *They have joy.*
> *They have dignity.*"
>
> ✍

I was mesmerized by her passion and sense of pride, as she revealed the view she saw—her family's history. Then we looked out at the clubhouse in the distance. Hanna began to describe this third scene by saying, "Look beyond what you see as the clubhouse, Lorraine. Out there, I see a long dirt road leading to the Big House. As I look down the road there is my grandmother. She is coming to work, committed to wash, cook, clean and care for the children in the big house. She is wearing a perfectly starched gray dress with an apron so white it seems to blind you in the sun. Can you see it, Lorraine? She walks with pride as she goes to work because she has a job.

On Fridays she has a special strut about her because she has just been paid and she is saving money for her children to go to college so they never have to wear a gray dress and white apron".

Then Hanna gives me a look that shows how much she admires and respects her grandmother. She continues her description. "In my grandmother's pocket is a fine silk hankie. Peach and teal. It is the only piece of finery she owns and she treasures it. It was given to her by one of the ladies she worked for."

Hanna paused and smiled, then she looked toward a very large home and began to describe the fourth scene: "If only you could see the smile on my mother's face as you look over there. I can clearly see my mom sitting on the porch of a big beautiful house. It is the home of her college classmate and they are studying for an exam. The family treats my mom like she is a member of their family. To my knowledge, they never acknowledged a difference in the color of her skin."

Having shown me the *real view*, one that I had completely missed because I had no way to appreciate the history, she then shared with me the story of her acquisition of the property.

"Several years ago," she began, "I learned the history of this land and the heritage of my ancestors. It was then that I became determined to own it and to create a resting place and a legacy for those four generations". It is by design that these benches have been placed by cool running brooks. This configuration gives us a beautiful place to rest and provides shelter from

the heat. These large trees have been invitingly placed to provide shade. We've planted an apple tree symbolic that none of the apples have to be given up or handed over to the owner of the land. We've taken special pleasure in creating a room filled with

soft, plush peach and teal cushions made of the finest silk, to give us a favorite place to sit. These ebony hand carved tables, symbolic of strength and endurance, made by my grandfather, adorn the perimeters. All of this is so special to me. *My* view from here", she said, "is filled with joy and humility."

Then Hanna looked at me with a smile and said, "Now, what is your view from here, Lorraine?

Why don't you call me in a few days and let's talk."

She continued by saying, "We all have a view. The Christians, Jews, American Indians, women, children of farmers, families of the poor, even those who live in the country who were teased by the children living in the city. We can, and should, all stand and look back at the progress that has been made."

Her story changed my way of seeing things. It changed my view of much of life and helped me recognize the importance of seeing through the eyes of clients, associates, peers, friends, family and even those with whom I disagreed. After all, isn't that the only way to really know how to offer your best recommendations or advice?

Now, I invite you to stand one more time and look around your world. Do you see anything that your grandparents could not have seen or enjoyed? Think about it. Maybe it is financial stability, confidence, an opportunity to enjoy a vocation or sit in a fine restaurant. Chances are, after hearing Hanna's description of her view, your view has changed. If so, I invite you from this day forward to enjoy "The View From Here" for all of your ancestors and friends who no longer are here to enjoy it.

Until you stand with the spirit of another, you simply cannot see what they see.

The Present of the Past

We all are profoundly impacted by the people in our past and the emotional and personal deposits they make in our life account. "The Present of the Past" is an inspirational presentation, delivered in story form that asks you to reflect on those who have contributed to your values, actions, beliefs and more. Be prepared to soul search a bit and enjoy a few moments of understanding the nature of gifts.

Do you think of what small actions or incidences in your past contribute to your today? Ask yourself: What "present," what "gift," has your past given you that lives with you today?

Regardless of whether we are aware of it or admit it, events, our reaction to events, and people in our past define:

1. Who we are
2. What we do
3. What we believe
4. How we act

In my eyes many of those events and many of the people associated with those events represent gifts I have received. And as I bundle those gifts in beautifully wrapped packages, they represent The Present Of The Past.

As I share four of them with you, I invite you to reflect on your own past and see what presents come into your awareness.

❧*Laura Mae—Mom*❧

My parents separated when I was very young and I was raised by my mom. Unfortunately when there is a single parent household, that parent has to serve as both emotional coach and disciplinarian. It is this parent's role to teach you the difference between right and wrong.

Whenever I did something that was pleasing to Mom, she did not hesitate to let me know. I can still hear her soft voice today saying "Lo, that's wonderful. I am pleased that you decided to take that on." Even though her words were clear and precise, it was actually her tone that spoke to me, relaying her message of love and encouragement.

But just as her gentle voice complimented, her stern voice reprimanded when she was displeased. If I had done something she did not find pleasing, or if she felt I had misbehaved, she would call me by my full name—"Lorraine Green, you know better than that."

Her gift? She taught me right from wrong.

❧Eddie Green—Dad❧

My dad did not really spend a great deal of time in my life until I was approaching my teens. He was a very soft-spoken person—always. Even though he wasn't a formally educated man, his goal was to make sure that I did my absolute best. In fact, he accepted no less than perfection from me.

When I was in high school and college, I can recall many occasions when I would share with him the results of exams. Often when they were returned with a score of 85 or 90, it was like 100 to me, because the work was very difficult. However, dad did not buy it. Regardless of the degree of difficulty, his response was always the same.

Never once did he accept less than perfection; never once did he allow me to accept it. Even when I started working in the corporate world and going through training programs, I remember the difficulty that I sometimes had in understanding the material. Even then, my dad would always say, in the same tone of voice, "99 ½ won't do. You gotta make a hundred."

He never settled for less, and passed that on to me.

Thus, from my dad came the gift of striving for excellence.

❦*Reverend Wise*❦

For a while, during my elementary school days, I lived in Prosperity, South Carolina with my grandparents. Yes, it was a very small town with a very optimistic, abundant name. As with all small towns, there was the neighborhood Black Baptist church—ours being Antioch Baptist Church. Every Sunday morning I would leave home wearing my Sunday best with seven cents tied in a corner of my white handkerchief—two pennies for the missionary offering and five cents for the regular offering. (I wasn't the biggest tither, but people said I was the cutest! And I was consistent.)

One Sunday, between Sunday school and church, I decided to sneak down the country road to a popular little sweet shop. I was so excited about the two peppermint sticks I bought for myself. They were only a penny each, and I still had two pennies for the missionary fund and three pennies left for the regular collection. I proudly placed the coins on the table as we marched up to the front of the church to give our offering.

After the service, Reverend Wise would always chat with the children. He possessed that powerful Pastoral Oratorical Voice which all masters of the pulpit seemed to have. He would:

• Encourage us to be honest, and
• Inspire us to "Let our little light shine."

As he began to talk he asked me questions:

- How is your mom doing in New York?

- How is school going?

- Do you have any questions you want to ask me?

- Any problems you want to talk about?

I was quick in my replies. "Oh, Reverend Wise, all is well. My mom is doing fine. I spoke to her this week. School is great. In fact, I am getting all A's."

Then seemingly right out of the heavens his strong penetrating Pastoral Voice rang out, "Have you robbed God lately?"

I felt as if the red from the peppermint sticks must have been smeared all over my face. Knowing I was caught red-handed (or red-faced, if I continue my thought about the peppermint sticks) I said, "No way, Reverend Wise! In fact, today God and I bought some peppermint sticks and we ate them together after Sunday school." (Not only was I cute, I could think on my feet!)

Reverend Wise looked down at me and in the strong pastoral voice which resonates across the room replied, "Ham-mercy child. Are you letting your little light shine? Are you being honest?"

No longer could I savor the sweet aftertaste of the peppermint—it was long gone. Though I wanted to correct him and inform him that he should say "*have* mercy," I knew this was not the time. (You see, I complemented my cuteness with diplomacy—and maybe even a little wisdom beyond my years!)

I also learned that day, though I did not welcome it at the time, that he had given me a timeless gift.

Reverend Wise gave me the gift of honesty.

❧ *Evelyn Brown* ❧
Better known as Aunt Evelyn

This is a gift I absolutely cherish. My 'life presents' would be incomplete without it. This gift was given to me by my colorful Aunt Evelyn. When I say colorful—take me literally. You see, Aunt Evelyn believed in enjoying the splendors of life. I can see her now:

- She had dark pretty brown skin.

- She sported a short, fashionable haircut, dyed red with blond tips in the top. (It may be my own idiosyncratic preferences at work, but don't you just love blond accents in red hair?)

- She was a waitress in the restaurant section of a bar in Harlem that was frequented by the "big money" men in Harlem.

- She was determined not to look like anyone else. Aunt Evelyn agreed to wear the required white

> *Live each day to the max. You only go around one time.*

uniform, but she chose white nylon instead of cotton. Did she have class or what? But she didn't stop there. Imagine this: Under her uniform she wore a red slip adorned in lace, along with a matching lace hanky in the breast pocket. Her personality and laugh captured everyone, and patrons filled the restaurant just to be in her presence.

- She was sexy—and she knew it.

Sometimes while visiting her, I would stretch out across her bed reveling in her stories about how she loved to dance. Then she would stand me up and spin me around as we danced around her bedroom. I felt like a princess. She delighted in showing me the gorgeous outfits she purchased to go dancing at the Savoy, a very well known Harlem Ballroom.

She loved living. I can see her now, posing with her hand resting on her curved hip, taking a long slow puff from her elegant black cigarette holder that was trimmed in gold, and telling me, "Lo, live every day to the max. You only go around one time, Sugar."

Thanks Aunt Evelyn for your gift—the joy of living.

It would seem that these presents can be easily forgotten, but that's not the case! You see, every day my 'presents' from the past come into play.

If I am tempted to "wing it" on an assigned task—I hear my dad saying, "99 ½ won't do. You gotta make a hundred." Immediately I start to prepare, to ensure I deliver the very best and highest quality training, proposal, or content possible. I claim the gift of striving for excellence.

There have been times when a clerk at a store or a teller at the bank has given me too much change, and my first thought is to grab the cash and run. But before I can even turn from the counter, I hear Reverend Wise's pastoral voice echoing, "Ham-mercy child. Always be honest, and let your little light shine." The Gift of Honesty stands before me, and I am compelled to do the right thing with no regrets.

We all are accustomed to those hourly-rates assignments which are paid or evaluated based on the amount of time required to complete the task. I must admit that I have been tempted to add ten minutes here and there to increase the time and the billable amount. However, the presence of Laura Mae, my dear mom, will just not allow me. If I come close to padding the bill, her voice rocks my world as I hear, "Lorraine Green. You know better." That precious gift of Right from Wrong.

Then there are those times when I allow myself to become heavy with the serious stuff of this life. Thank goodness for the joyful laugh of Aunt Evelyn, coming before me saying, "Lo, live each day to the max. You only go around once, Sugar." The amazing gift - Enjoy Life.

With my treasured and beautifully wrapped "present" intact, carefully packed and ready for life, I joyfully take it with me into my future.

I don't know what life gifts you may have received in your Past that comprise your Present. And I don't know which of these gifts you wish to take into your future. But before this week is over, take a few moments to recall and jot down the special gifts you have received. (It will take a few minutes to organize your thoughts and capture them in writing, but I encourage you to take the time to do it. You will be glad you did.)

Keep in mind that you do not have to accept every gift that has been given! You can give yourself permission to say "No thank you. I will not accept that."

But, for all of those gifts of the past that are making a positive impact on your present, keep them. Cherish them. Open them often and savor their value.

For all those gifts of the past that are having a negative impact on your present, throw them away. Do not give them any more energy.

Remember—as you celebrate your present—and anticipate your future—joyfully take with you each of those selected gifts beautifully wrapped as your **PRESENT OF THE PAST.**

Life's Like A Bubble

Sitting on the front step of the apartment building where he lived, Timothy, now three years old, longed to see his dad. Shortly after the celebration of his second birthday his father had left without even a farewell, leaving a hole in Timothy's spirit. Though Timothy did not remember many of the details of living with his dad, he vividly remembered the bubbles he and his father used to blow and how he always tried to catch them and save them. They would strive to blow bubbles faster and faster so that they could have a lot of bubbles, but they still did not last. They just floated away or disappeared as they popped.

We know that bubbles do not last, and that was something Timothy was to learn.

He remembered his dad and dearly missed him. When he was with his dad he was happy, I guess we can say "bubbly." But he was sometimes frustrated with how much energy went into making the bubbles they enjoyed, only to see them disappear so quickly. Often he would cry repeating, "Make 'um stay. Make 'um stay." Now that his dad was gone, this cry had a double meaning. He longed for both the bubbles and his dad to stay in his life.

Timothy's mother, Anna, realizing the hole in her son's spirit, did everything in her power to cheer him up. She watched him experience periods of happiness and joy, only to find the veil of sadness overwhelming him again. Every day after she picked him up from daycare, they would sit on the steps and blow bubbles. He still thrilled at trying to catch them. However, by now he was beginning to realize that he could never save them. They were simply brief moments of joy.

When Timothy was about to enter the first grade, an uncle visited him with a special gift, plastic bubbles. As he un-wrapped his gift, Timothy saw a tube that resembled a toothpaste tube, and a straw that was somewhat shorter than the ones he used for his chocolate milk. "Look Timothy. Now you can blow bubbles that last. You can make them as large as you want, and keep them for a whole day. Some may last for two days or three days. You can even hold them in your hands and play with them."

Timothy watched as his uncle opened the tube containing the magic bubbles, squeezed a small amount of the plastic onto his finger, and placed it on one end the small straw that he had just removed from the box. The other end he placed between his lips and began to blow. As he blew, a tiny bubble about the size of a pea started to form.

Almost without breathing Timothy watched as the bubble continued to take shape on the end of the small straw. As he continued to blow, it began to take the shape of a jellybean and became translucent. A few more breaths and the jelly bean was the size of an egg, and then a tennis ball. With excitement and anticipation, Timothy's eyes seemed to grow at the same rate as the bubble. Soon the bubble was as large as a football and still growing. Timothy wanted to yell "Stop. Don't let it pop", but he was too mesmerized.

After a few more breaths, his uncle removed his lips from one end of the straw and the bubble from the other, pinching the disconnected end of the bubble sealed it to keep the air inside. Passing it to Timothy he saw the happiest of faces with large brown eyes staring in amazement. "Will it pop?" Timothy asked. "Not right away" stated his uncle. "It's a loving bubble and will stay as long as it can. When it does have to leave, just remember, you can always make another. Isn't that magnificent?"

His uncle was right. The bubble lasted for over two days and Timothy kept it with him every waking moment.

At the end of the second day he asked his mom if his dad would stay longer too when he came back. It was painfully obvious that he associated the quick short lived relationship with his dad with the quick short lived relationship with his bubbles. Unfortunately, she could not give the answer that he wanted most to hear.

Years passed and Timothy grew into manhood. As he moved on to his professional career, he often thought of the times in his life when he felt like he was still chasing bubbles. However, they now took on a different meaning. They no longer represented the evasiveness of a fragile translucent object, nor the father that he never saw again. They began to represent lost moments, missed goals, escaped opportunities, and failed plans.

When he was a child, his mother often explained that even though the bubbles will pop, he did have time to appreciate them and see the rainbow image within. Her intention was to help him develop an appreciation of the "now", and not focus on the regrets of temporary existences or situations. She realized the importance that this belief would have as he went through life. He could now reflect on his mom's actions with appreciation.

One day on the radio he heard the song "I'm Forever Blowing Bubbles", a song composed in 1918 by James Kendis, James Brockman and Nat Vincent. Timothy immediately felt a kindred spirit with the composers. This song, which debuted in the musical "The Passing Show", speaks of the dreams, schemes, hopes, and desires that come to our minds then float away, only to return and have the cycle repeated. The words played in his mind.

> *I'm forever blowing bubbles,*
> *Pretty bubbles in the air.*
> *They fly so high,*

Nearly reach the sky,
Then like my dreams,
They fade and die.

If we can begin to see our moments in this manner, we realize that each is fragile, beautiful, contains a rainbow and will not be with us for long. Knowing this, why not pause, truly experience it, cherish it, celebrate it and allow it to register as a memory. So often we forget to celebrate the moment because we're rushing off to attend the next meeting, complete a pending task, plan for the next career enhancement or network with the 'right person'. Stop. Savor the beauty of your moment. Take a mental picture that will store as a cherished memory.

- What is surrounding you?
- What feelings are present?
- Who is sharing it with you?

Often the moment seems too insignificant to mention. Then years later we realize that it was a life mini-highlight and the cherished memory will last forever.

> *We cannot hold on to things that are not meant to stay.*

You see, for years Timothy had been learning valuable lessons in life, but was really too young to realize it. In the beginning when he cried because of the disappearing bubble, he was displaying disappointment. However, as Timothy grew up, he realized that he could not hold on to things that were not meant to stay. Just as in the song, they would fade away.

Thanks to his uncle he learned that some things, even bubbles, are designed to last longer, to be with us for a while. However, even they are temporary. He learned to appreciate the moments of his day and not allow the thoughts of next business meeting to overpower his relationships and family. He learned that many things are beautiful even if they only last for a minute. He grew to appreciate life.

What about you? Can you relate to Timothy's experiences? Even more significantly, can you benefit from Timothy's story? As a family man with three children, Timothy has made it a point to experience life, to spend time with family, to be present for every possible moment and to teach his family to do the same. He realizes that some experiences are short lived and float away into the air, while others, more like the plastic bubbles, can be handled and shaped to allow us to enjoy them for a while. His commitment is to appreciate and experience every Life Bubble that comes his way.

Timothy and I hope you do the same!

Thank You

I cannot express to you how much I truly appreciate your sharing my experiences with me. The most important part, however, would be that my testimonies awakens in you your testimonies of life. If so, share them with someone. You never know how they will be impacted.

As this wonderful life would have it, two weeks before this book was scheduled to go to press, I received two notes on Facebook that just solidified the message of "Ripples" and "Who's Defining You?." I would like to share them with you.

Hi Lorraine- I just completed a survey for Duke Professional Development and when asked to add a comment I told them about the phenomenal orator, motivator and inspirational woman you are and have been in our sessions. I'll never forget you.

Armetta Hamlett

Thank you for the advice you gave me years ago during my time at IBM and on our very first lunch together. "Never let anyone tell you how far you can go and how well you can do in life; you hold the keys to your success; and always surround yourself with people with vision and purpose." The very thing you told me about people's perception of you is a mantra my children live by to this day. "There will come a day when people will stop listening at what you say, but watch what you do". To some measure, I hope I have lived up to those ideals you set in motion some twenty-plus years ago.

Four kids later, two in undergrad, one in law at UNC and oh yes; our two year Meaghan, I want you to know your words of encouragement did not fall upon deaf ears. Thank you for being an example.
All my love,

Sonne Mullins Barnes

The unsolicited testimonies of these two ladies came at the precise moment in life when they mean so much. Thank you Sonne and Armetta for your confirming words.

I hope that I will have an opportunity to meet many of you who have read my books and to speak for your organization to share my messages. Feel free to contact me—even if just to say hello.

Sincerely,

Lorraine

Lorraine@lorrainestephens.com

919 876-3100

About the Author

As an author and speaker Lorraine Stephens has the pleasure of speaking on overcoming obstacles and finding our "sweet-spot" of life. This is delivered through real life stories and experiences. She is a Speaker Extraordinaire— blending empathy, humor, and information.

For more than seventeen years Lorraine Stephens has delivered presentations, seminars and keynote addresses to corporations, educators, and business associations. With her focus on assisting others to step into their power, her topics have ranged from valuable technical information, to confidence building, to team work.

Having authored three books and co-authored two more, she knows the significance of sharing her technical skills as well as her personal insights in a relatable manner.

Lorraine is a member of several speakers' organizations including

- **Toastmasters International,**
- **National Speakers Association**
- **International Speakers Network**
- **Raleigh Speakers Bureau**

Let her keynote take your next event to its peak!

Lorraine Stephens
6040-A Six Forks Road, #323
Raleigh, NC 27609
919 876-3100

Lorraine@lorrainestephens.com
www.lorrainestephens.com
www.lorrainespeaks.com

Notes

Story	Notes	Date

Story	Notes	Date